Scottish Art

Contents

What is Art?

Art is a way of communicating, just like talking, writing, singing and shouting.

Art is about imagination.

Art is a way of responding to our environment.

Anybody can be an artist. All of us can respond in our own ways to what we see around us – no one way is 'correct'. Because everyone can be creative, the world of art is full of variety, where all our ideas and opinions are of value.

What is art about?

Art can be about anything at all - anything people are interested in.

There are lots of different subjects in art. Here are some of the best ones:

People – ordinary people, famous people, unusual people;

Places – wild places, busy places, beautiful places;

Things – things we collect, things we make, things we find interesting;

Stories – stories we tell, stories we hear, stories we can't put into words;

Dreams – fantasies, visions, imaginary worlds.

In this book, we look at how artists in the past have dealt with these subjects, and how, nowadays, there are many new and different approaches.

What is art made of?

In the past, artists mainly used oil paint for pictures, and stone, wood and clay for sculpture. Nowadays, art can be made out of almost anything, such as plastic, metal, cardboard or glass. Artists can use all sorts of unexpected materials to make their work: junk from a scrapyard, things they have found on the beach, old tyres, bricks, twigs, even snow.

Art is not just paintings and sculptures. It can be printed or photographed, welded or woven, made on a computer or made with a video.

Looking at

Cover picture: *The Glen Burn*, 1987, by Duncan Shanks
(see page 16).
Inside cover picture: *Sidewinder*, 1985, by Andy Goldsworthy
(see page 19).
Above: detail from *Glencoe*, 1864, by Horatio McCulloch
(see page 20).

First published in 1996 by Wayland (Publishers) Ltd
61 Western Road, Hove, East Sussex BN3 1JD, England

© Copyright 1996 Wayland (Publishers) Ltd

British Library Cataloguing in Publication Data
McGeoch, Brian
    Looking at Scottish Art
    I. Title II. Porch, Steven
    709.411

ISBN 0-7502-1749-9

Editor: Katrina Maitland Smith
Consultant: Ishbel Maclean, Senior Producer, Educational
    Television, BBC Education Scotland
Picture research: Shelley Noronha
Concept design: Derek Lee
Book design: Pardoe Blacker Ltd
Printed and bound by B.P.C. Paulton Books Ltd

Acknowledgement
The publishers wish to thank Strathclyde Regional Council
Department of Education for their invaluable assistance with
this book.

Picture Acknowledgements
The publishers also wish to thank the following for allowing their
pictures to be used in this book: Artbridge/Mhairi Killin 23; Boyle
Family 18; City of Aberdeen Art Gallery & Museums Collections 6
(detail), 15, 28; Calum Colvin 34; Cyril Gerber Fine Art, Glasgow
10; Robin Gillanders 11; Glasgow Museums: Art Gallery and
Museum, Kelvingrove *title and contents page picture* (detail), 13, 20, 21,
22, 32, 38, 39; Andy Goldsworthy *endpapers*, 19; James Herd/David
A. Annand 12; Ellen Howden/Glasgow Museums 36; © Hunterian
Art Gallery, University of Glasgow 24; Shona Kinloch 30; Andrew
Miller/Nicola Atkinson-Griffith 31; John Mooney 37; National
Gallery of Scotland 14, 26, 33; Amy Neville 7 (detail), 17; Elizabeth
Ogilvie 25; Scotland in Focus (G. Leaper) 8, (RW) 8–9, (RM203) 9;
Scottish National Gallery of Modern Art 27; Duncan Shanks *cover
picture*, 16; © Summerlee Heritage Trust 6–7 (main picture); © D.C.
Thomson & Co. Ltd, *The Beano* 29; © Adrian Wiszniewski and the
Glasgow Print Studio 35.
Map artwork on pg 43 by Sallie Alane Reason; labels by Hardlines.

Is art difficult to understand?

When people talk about art, they use words like abstract, composition, form, harmony, texture and tone. It helps to get to know some of these words because they crop up quite often.

Artists also use a lot of technical words to tell us how they make their work: words like screenprint, relief, construction and installation.

Fortunately, it is not necessary to remember all of these. As you read about works of art in this book, words that need some explaining are shown in bold the first time they are used, and the explanation is given in the Glossary on pages 40-41.

The most important thing is that we enjoy art. The best way to do this is to look at a work of art, try to decide what it is about and whether we like it or not, talk about it, and have an opinion. If we do this, most art is easy to understand and enjoy.

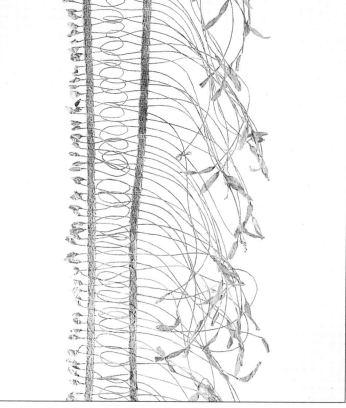

Artists today use all sorts of materials for their art.
Main picture: David Mach at work on *Whirl* (see page 23).
Inset left: detail from Will Maclean's *Leviathan Elegy* (page 28).
Right: detail from Amy Neville's Wall hanging (page 17).

What is Scottish art?

Wherever they live in the world, all artists respond to their surroundings. The Scottish environment – its landscape, its weather, its architecture, its people – have inspired artists for hundreds of years. In this book, all the art is by people who live or work in Scotland. Looking at their ideas can help us to understand more about the country and its people.

Across the centuries, Scottish artists have watched and commented on events and changes in their way of life. In the nineteenth century, large numbers of Scots were forced to leave their homes and go abroad during the Highland Clearances. This great change was recorded by many Scottish artists. In the twentieth century, artists have created works that make us think more deeply about what happened during the First and Second World Wars.

The way we live and how we look are also good subjects for making art. Poor children playing in the dirty streets of a big city in the 1950s before slum houses were cleared to make way for new homes, or the vanished way of life

of whalers from tiny fishing villages working thousands of miles out in the stormy Atlantic Ocean are examples of the many subjects that have fascinated artists.

No part of Scottish life has been left untouched by artists. Looking at the hustle and bustle of city life, with its cluttered streets, busy

Art is a way of responding to our surroundings and changing ways of life.
(Pictured left, Victoria Dock, Aberdeen Harbour;
above, Grangemouth Oil Refinery;
top right, Inverailort, West Highlands.)

Making art

Art is a world of amazing variety. People, places, things, stories and dreams are just some of the possible subjects that we can explore as artists. Art can express our ideas and emotions: it can calm us, it can shock us, it can change our minds.

Looking at art is enjoyable, but making our own art is even better. It is only when we are drawing, painting or printing, producing sculptures or building constructions that we truly understand the thoughts and ideas behind works of art made by others. Choosing the subject, gathering information about it, deciding which materials to use, then developing the ideas, are all part of the process of making a work of art. It can be fun, it can be messy, it can be very exciting and sometimes it can be difficult but, by doing this, we will be communicating, in our own way, how we feel about the world.

traffic and polluted environment, has inspired artists to produce works of art of amazing cleverness and beauty. Modern technology, with all its benefits and drawbacks, is an important aspect of our lives, which many artists are now exploring.

The delicate balance between the hi-tech world of industry and the beautiful and varied environment we have inherited gives artists working today the chance to comment on and respond to their surroundings in new and exciting ways.

People

Artists have always been interested in making pictures of people. In the days before cameras, artists were often employed to paint **portraits** of their wealthy **patrons**. They had to be very skilful to make their **subjects** look as life-like as possible. Nowadays, anyone can be the subject of a work of art, whether they are rich or poor, young or old, famous or unknown. Artists are now interested in more than just a **likeness**: they can look at how a person feels, whether they are angry or calm, happy or sad. They might want to explore someone's personality, or show how someone lives or works.

LESLEY BANKS

Lesley Banks is an artist who likes to make oil paintings of the interesting people she knows. This one is a picture of her friend, Nancy, doing the washing-up after breakfast. Nancy is standing at the sink, with the sunlight coming in through the kitchen window.

This painting is just one of a whole set of pictures about the same woman. The artist was interested in showing Nancy's **character**, and she spent a long time visiting Nancy at home, making drawings, taking photographs and finding out more about her subject.

In this painting, Nancy seems happy and contented in her bright, sunny kitchen. Her face is calm, with a hint of a smile. She seems to be deep in thought, and the artist has shown this by making an **image** of quiet **harmony**. The **balance** of light and shadow, and the soft **colours** – warm yellows, reds and browns – help to create this relaxed **atmosphere**.

After Breakfast, 1995,
by Lesley Banks
(born 1962),
oil on **canvas**, 74 x 99cm.
Collection: Cyril Gerber.

ROBIN GILLANDERS

Robin Gillanders is an artist who uses a camera to make pictures of people, but his photographs are not just simple **snapshots**. They are portraits, carefully **composed** to tell us a lot about the personality of the subject. Robin Gillanders likes to photograph interesting people and, just like a portrait painter, he spends time finding out about them. He takes lots of pictures, trying to work out the best way of creating the right **mood**. The choice of black and white, in which **tones** softly merge from dark to light, helps us to see the **shapes** and **forms** in his work.

This is his portrait of George, the 'lollipop man' at the local primary school. Instead of showing him at work, helping children across the road, Robin Gillanders decided to photograph him at home, relaxing with a cup of tea. The picture tells us quite a lot about George. He looks like a nice, cheerful kind of man who is probably a grandfather. He has a child's painting on his fridge door, a teddy bear in a pram and even a small model of a 'lollipop lady'. George's face is in the centre of the picture and his eyes are looking straight at us. His mouth is open, as if he is in the middle of telling a story.

George Hughes, 1995, by Robin Gillanders (born 1952), photograph. Collection: the artist.

Nae Day Sae Dark, 1989, by David A. Annand (born 1948), cast resin and stainless steel. Collection: Perth and Kinross District Council.

Rather than making a flat, **two-dimensional** picture, like a drawing, a painting or a photograph, some artists like to create **three-dimensional** works to focus on the shape and form of something.

In this **sculpture** by David Annand, two figures are leaning against the inside of a big metal ring, which appears, rather strangely, to be floating in mid-air. On the inside of the ring is a poem. The sculpture is good fun and quite puzzling. Is the ring supporting the two figures, or are they holding up the ring? Why is one of the figures wearing a blindfold?

The **life-size** figures have been **cast** in **resin** and are very **realistic**, with lots of **detail** in their faces, their hair and in their clothes. The rough **textures** of the figures **contrast** with the smooth surface of the ring.

The artist has taken a small moment, perhaps from a game of blind man's buff, and frozen it in time for us to look at, think about, and even be part of. The sculpture stands in the middle of a busy town centre. All around, people go about their business, sometimes stopping to talk and even leaning on the sculpture, becoming part of it, just like the figures themselves.

JOHN BELLANY

Painting a picture of yourself, known as a **self-portrait**, is one way of exploring the sort of person you are. It is a good way of explaining your feelings to others: your moods, your hopes, your fears.

John Bellany painted a whole **series** of pictures of himself, starting at a time in his life when he became very ill with liver disease. The title of this picture comes from a legend in Greek mythology: Prometheus stole fire from the gods, who punished him by sending an eagle to eat his liver, night after night. In this painting, John Bellany has illustrated the strong emotions he was feeling during his long illness. He shows himself as a figure with two mask-like faces, representing his own struggle between life and death.

The artist has produced a painting full of energy, with its wild **brushstrokes** and vivid colours. It gives us no idea of what the artist looks like, but tells us all about the torture he was going through. The staring eyes, the glinting teeth and the open wounds draw us into the artist's terrifying world. By painting in such an **expressive** way, he has shown us some of the deepest, darkest feelings that people can experience.

Prometheus II, 1988, by John Bellany (born 1942), oil on canvas, 173 x 152cm. Collection: Glasgow Museums, Art Gallery and Museum, Kelvingrove.

13

Henry Raeburn was the most famous portrait painter of his day. He painted many of Scotland's important people, such as politicians, judges and landowners. The subject of this portrait, Colonel Alastair Macdonnell of Glengarry, was the chief of a Scottish Highland clan. To show off his power, the Colonel asked Raeburn to paint his portrait showing him in his full ceremonial dress.

In this picture, we see the young chief standing proudly in his splendid tartan costume, with his daggers and his gun. The swords and shields hanging on the wall behind tell us more about the war-like history of his clan. His complicated outfit looks as if it must have taken a very long time to paint but, when you look closely at the picture (see the detail below), you can see that it has been quickly painted with broad brushstrokes. Raeburn was famous for his ability to make his portraits very realistic with just a few strokes of paint. He was also admired for the way he used light in his work. Here, Colonel Macdonnell's face is lit by a golden light, while the rest of the scene is dark and shadowy. This strong contrast between light and dark makes the picture more dramatic.

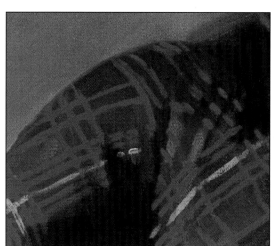

Colonel Alastair Macdonnell of Glengarry, c. 1812, by Sir Henry Raeburn RA, RSA (1756–1823), oil on canvas, 241 x 150cm. Collection: National Gallery of Scotland.

JOAN EARDLEY

Some Scottish artists of the past liked to look at ordinary people as the **inspiration** for their art. In *Brother and Sister*, we can see the work of an artist who was fascinated by scenes of everyday life. In the 1950s, Joan Eardley spent her time among the old, run-down tenements and streets of Glasgow. She made **sketches** and took photographs as **studies** to help her when she composed and painted her pictures.

This picture shows a young girl with her older brother. We can easily imagine what is happening: the boy has been sent to the corner shop for a pint of milk, and has been told to bring his sister home for tea after she has been playing in the street. Joan Eardley's work is very expressive. It shows how much she understood about the hard lives of poor children in a big city. The picture is roughly painted in thick strokes of strong, earthy colour, contrasting with patches of bright red and blue. She has captured the mood of this scene perfectly: the children's scruffy clothes, the way the big brother has hold of his younger sister's arm, and the **graffiti** chalked on the tenement wall behind all help to build up the atmosphere of the picture.

Brother and Sister, 1955, by Joan Eardley (1921–63), oil on canvas, 102 x 76cm. Collection: City of Aberdeen Art Gallery & Museums Collections.

Places

Making works of art about the world we live in can help us to understand and learn more about our environment. This kind of subject in art is often called a **landscape**. It allows artists not only to show what places look like, but also to express their opinions and tell us how they feel about what they see. Changes in the seasons, in weather and light have an effect both on the landscape we look at and on the emotions we feel.

DUNCAN SHANKS

Duncan Shanks enjoys living in the countryside and often visits the same place day after day to make drawings and **pastel** sketches as studies for his finished paintings.

In *The Glen Burn*, he shows us one of his favourite spots, where a small stream rushes over rocks, creating little pools and waterfalls. He has not made an exact copy of what he saw. Instead, he has used all his senses to respond to the experience he had there. The stream tumbles down from the top of the picture through light pinks, greens and reds. The **lines** flow, suggesting the way the water tumbles and falls. The middle of the picture is filled with round stones, which are sometimes shown as outlines, sometimes as solid shapes painted with splashes of vibrant yellow, orange and red. At the bottom of the picture things become more realistic: we can see the water foaming through the leaves and twigs. In some parts, the paint is spread thickly with a knife; in other parts it is spread thinly with a big, wide brush. The whole feeling is one of excitement, where the artist is expressing directly his delight in the landscape he loves.

The Glen Burn, 1987, by Duncan Shanks (born 1937), oil on canvas, 147 x 193cm.
Private collection.

16

AMY NEVILLE

Amy Neville was born in a small village in the Scottish Highlands, but it was only when she came to live in a big city that she realized how much the countryside meant to her. The artist's work reflects and echoes nature, highlighting the beauty of the landscape. She makes three-dimensional **textiles**, **embroideries** and weavings, which are inspired by the landscape and the structures she finds growing in nature. Her **constructions** are made from natural materials such as cotton, linen or paper.

In this wall hanging, though the delicate leaves appear to be real, they are actually made from fine paper, which has been carefully rolled and twisted to copy the texture and look of real leaves. Hundreds of these paper 'leaves' have been woven into thin bands of linen cloth to make a fragile structure, which seems as if it could have grown naturally. When works like this are shown in an art gallery, they give us a strong sense of the countryside with its changing seasons of growth and decay.

Wall hanging (untitled), 1995,
by Amy Neville (born 1973),
paper and linen.
Collection: the artist.

The Boyle Family work on each piece of art together: mother, father, daughter and son. They share their ideas and reasons for choosing the place they want to make a work of art about. Their view of the landscape is unusual because they look very closely at a scene and make an exact three-dimensional copy of what they see, which is correct in every detail.

They are mainly interested in towns, especially the surface of the ground. They like the many textures they find in crumbling concrete, smooth tiles or rusty metal. They even show the smallest speck of dust.

In *Road Work Study*, although the cast-iron drains and heavy cobblestones appear to be real objects, the whole construction is made of lightweight plastic and can be easily lifted by two people. It is very surprising to see a work like this in an art gallery because it looks like a chunk of ground brought in from outside. In taking a place away from its normal surroundings, the Boyle Family draw our attention to the interest of ordinary landscapes, which we would usually pass by without noticing.

Road Work Study (Urban Renewal, Glasgow), 1990, by the Boyle Family (Mark born 1934, Joan b.1936, Sebastian b.1962, Georgia b.1964), painted fibreglass, 213 x 548cm. Collection: Glasgow Museums, Art Gallery and Museum, Kelvingrove.

ANDY GOLDSWORTHY

Sidewinder, 1985, by Andy Goldsworthy (born 1956), wood. Grizedale Forest, Cumbria.

Most of Andy Goldsworthy's work can only be seen in the countryside where it is made. He makes constructions from the natural materials that he finds at the places he works: things like grass, leaves and stones, and sometimes even water, snow or ice.

When he visits a place, he likes to make changes to whatever he finds there. His work is never meant to last a long time. It is blown away or it melts, rots or becomes overgrown. All that remains is a photograph as proof that it ever existed.

In making *Sidewinder*, Andy Goldsworthy looked for trees that had been bent by the strength of the wind. It must have taken a great deal of effort to gather all the right shapes of trees to make the work. He enjoys searching for his materials because it means that he spends long hours in the environment he likes best. The finished sculpture looks like a giant, wavy wooden snake, weaving its way between the growing trees. It is a most unexpected form to find in a forest, and yet it is made from the forest itself.

HORATIO McCULLOCH

Over a hundred years ago, adventure stories about the Scottish Highlands were very popular with people who lived in the big cities. These people wanted to see the countryside that was described in the books they were reading. Because of this, landscape painting was widely enjoyed at the time.

This picture by Horatio McCulloch shows us the rough countryside of Glencoe in the north of Scotland, with its huge mountains, dark skies and herds of deer running wild. When we look at this painting we are left in no doubt about how grand and exciting this landscape is. There is no peaceful stillness in the picture. The howling wind, tumbling clouds and swirling mists give the feeling that Glencoe is a wild and dangerous place. The rich browns and warm yellows of the heather and bracken contrast with the glimpses of fresh, cool blues in the sky. This large, dramatic picture captures what it must feel like to stand in front of such an impressive scene.

Glencoe, 1864, by Horatio McCulloch (1805–67),
oil on canvas, 110 x 183cm.
Collection: Glasgow Museums, Art Gallery and Museum, Kelvingrove.

JOHN DUNCAN FERGUSSON

Damaged Destroyer, 1918, by John Duncan Fergusson (1874–1961), oil on canvas, 73.5 x 76cm.
Collection: Glasgow Museums, Art Gallery and Museum, Kelvingrove.

The countryside is not the only place artists are interested in. Looking at the city, with its buildings, streets and factories, can give us lots of ideas for making art. John Duncan Fergusson enjoyed painting this kind of subject. In *Damaged Destroyer*, he has looked at the ships and cranes in a dockyard and simplified the scene using circles, triangles and squares. Everything looks very solid; even the reflections in the water and the shadows on the buildings become important shapes in the **composition**.

Fergusson also loved working with colour and, in this painting, the soft blue of the ships and the sky makes a good contrast with the rusty orange on the side of the destroyer and the bright yellow of the masts in the middle of the picture. Although we can still recognize the shapes of ships, the artist has not tried to show the dockyard in a realistic way. Instead, he has used colour to make the shapes stand out against one another, and the result is a more **abstract** picture.

Things

Looking at objects as the inspiration for art gives us an ideal opportunity to play around with and explore shapes and colours, **patterns** and textures without the subject moving or changing. This type of subject is called **still life**. It gives us a chance to create compositions by choosing and arranging things any way we like.

ELIZABETH BLACKADDER

Wild Flowers, 1993, by Elizabeth Blackadder (born 1931), watercolour, 49 x 62cm. Collection: Glasgow Museums, Art Gallery and Museum, Kelvingrove.

Fresh flowers and clear glass vases are the kinds of things Elizabeth Blackadder likes to paint most. These objects are fragile and delicate and, because of this, the artist often uses **watercolour** paint, which is transparent and allows the white paper to shine through. Painting in watercolour requires great skill and confidence since the artist cannot easily make changes or paint over mistakes.

In this picture, the simple beauty of the wild flowers has been captured by the artist's sensitive use of line and colour. The soft reds, pinks and pale purples of the flowers go pleasingly with the faded green of the leaves. The glass vases and the water in them are painted with just a few strokes of see-through grey and light yellow.

Blackadder not only paints the objects she has chosen in a realistic way, she also takes great care over where each one is placed on the paper. Her compositions always have balance and harmony.

DAVID MACH

Instead of arranging objects as still lifes, some artists use them to make new works of art. David Mach is an artist who likes to take ordinary things, like coat-hangers, car tyres, even container trucks, and make sculptures from them. He uses objects that have been thrown away, and gives them a new meaning by turning them into something unusual.

His work makes us think about the things we keep and the things we throw away. His sculpture *Whirl* is in an industrial museum and uses the kinds of things you might find in such a place. Old cars and bits of machinery are caught up in a giant avalanche of newspapers, which looks as if it has poured into the museum through an open door. Although the artist has taken great care in placing each newspaper and piece of machinery, the whole work looks like one big accident. There are lots of ideas and questions behind this work. Is he saying something about the way objects are shown in museums; about technology being swept away by time; or is he just trying to make us laugh?

Whirl, 1995,
by David Mach (born 1956),
newspapers, found objects.
Collection: Summerlee
Heritage Trust, Coatbridge.

Doors, 1977, by Eduardo Paolozzi (born 1924), cast aluminium, four doors, each door 365 x 91cm. Collection: Hunterian Art Gallery, University of Glasgow.

Modern life has provided us with an enormous variety of new things to use as inspiration for art. Even the insides of objects like televisions, videos and computers become good sources of ideas for works. Eduardo Paolozzi is an artist who is inspired by images from electronics, engineering and architecture in our technological age. He uses his imagination to invent shapes that remind us of complex machines, mechanical robots and futuristic cities.

In *Doors* he has used these ideas to make a **relief** sculpture for the entrance to a museum. The curvy wires, boxy rectangles, and spinning wheels are **moulded** in gleaming, silvery metal to produce an abstract design that is all about the world we live in today.

Although Paolozzi has used these modern things as the start of his idea, the composition is the most important part of the work. The placing of the shapes, the way they fit together and the spaces between them are very carefully thought out. Each small part of the work is busy with interest, circle balanced against square, rectangle against curve. The whole complicated design comes together to make an exciting image of our hi-tech world.

ELIZABETH OGILVIE

Investigating and recording the things that interest us can help us to understand and enjoy our world. Drawing is one of the best ways of doing this. It is a simple method of making a picture, yet it allows us to say so much.

Elizabeth Ogilvie is an artist who looks at every detail of an object, drawing what she sees in a very realistic way, using only black and white. She enlarges the thing she is drawing to an enormous size, as if she has looked at it through a magnifying glass.

In *Place of the Issuing of Waves*, she has collected a group of objects from a beach and drawn each one separately on a very large **scale**. The tangled seaweed in the centre of the picture has been recorded in such detail that we can see every twist and turn it takes. This is contrasted by the smooth roundness of the egg-shaped pebbles on either side.

By changing the size of things and leaving out the colour, the artist is bringing to our attention the subtle textures of natural forms.

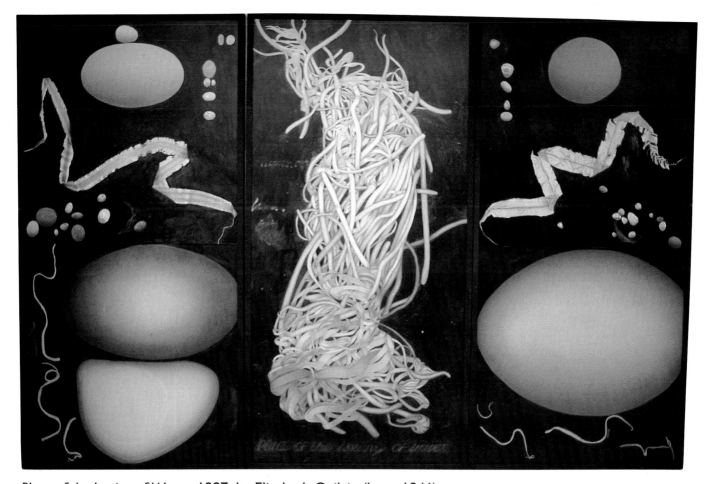

Place of the Issuing of Waves, 1987, by Elizabeth Ogilvie (born 1946), ink, **graphite**, pencil and crayon on paper, 244 x 366cm. Collection: the artist.

Painting still life pictures has been popular for hundreds of years. Natural, organic things such as fish, flowers and fruit eventually rot, but artists can show these things at their best. In the past, people liked the idea of capturing nature and placing it in a picture frame.

A pile of vegetables spread out on an old wooden table is a very ordinary subject, yet William MacGregor's painting makes us realize how interesting and even beautiful these simple things are. Although the still life looks very realistic, the detail (right) shows that it is painted with quite bold brushstrokes of thick oil paint. This **style** suits the rough, lumpy vegetables with the soil still clinging to them. The earthy colours of the table, the baskets and potatoes contrast with the rich greens, purples and reds of the cabbages, leeks and rhubarb. The arrangement of vegetables stands out against the plain white wall in the background and everything looks fresh and ready to eat.

The Vegetable Stall, 1884, by William York MacGregor (1855–1923), oil on canvas, 105 x 150cm. Collection: National Gallery of Scotland.

ANNE REDPATH

When Anne Redpath looked at things, she enjoyed the patterns and shapes they made when she laid them out to paint. Rather than making a realistic picture of each individual thing, she was more interested in the shapes created between the objects. Her paintings are more about making colourful arrangements, where the background is just as important as the objects themselves.

In *The Indian Rug*, she took objects, such as the chair, slippers and patterned rug, and used them only as a starting point. She made the colours stronger and simplified the shapes so that her picture became less realistic. The chair is a brilliant red, which contrasts with the white rug and the black floor. The broad bands of flat colour in the background help us to notice the busy, brightly-coloured **decorative** shapes in the rug. By making the objects into shapes, with each one fitting into the next like a jigsaw puzzle, her painting became a beautiful, almost abstract composition.

The Indian Rug, 1942, by Anne Redpath (1895–1965), oil on plywood, 73 x 96cm.
Collection: Scottish National Gallery of Modern Art.

Stories

For thousands of years, from the time of cave paintings to the comic books of today, artists have been involved in telling visual stories. This kind of art is sometimes known as **narrative**, and it has always been popular with Scottish artists. The subject for such works can range from simple stories about individual people to great **sagas** about whole communities.

WILL MACLEAN

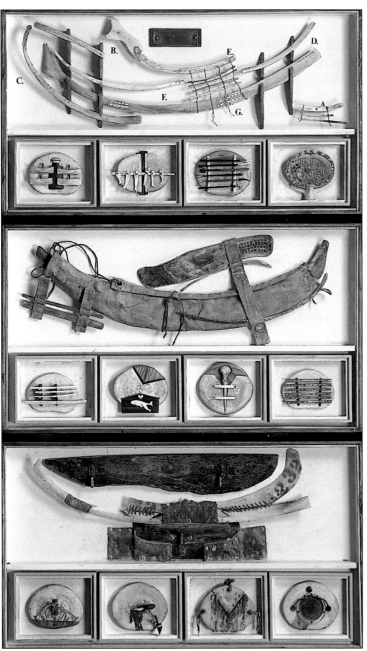

The artist Will Maclean was born in the north of Scotland. He uses the Highland tradition of telling stories as the inspiration for most of his work. He likes to work with mixed **media**, which means using different materials like wood, paint and ink, and sometimes includes objects that he has found or collected.

Will Maclean uses visual images the way a poet would use words, hinting at the tales he wants to tell. *Leviathan Elegy* is a story about people who used to hunt whales. The construction is arranged like a display case in a museum, each little composition contained within its own box. One compartment includes bones and pieces of wood that have been carved and assembled to remind us of the hull of a ship. In another box there are pieces of canvas and bone that strangely echo the shape of a whale. The weather-beaten look of the objects reminds us of the raging storms and crashing waves that might have rubbed them smooth. Throughout the work, there is a strong sense of a way of life that no longer exists.

Leviathan Elegy, 1982,
by Will Maclean (born 1941),
painted whalebone and found objects,
203 x 137cm.
Collection: City of Aberdeen Art Gallery &
Museums Collections.

DAVID SUTHERLAND

Cartoons are one of the most popular forms of modern art, and the stories they tell are known around the world. This comic page, by **graphic** artist David Sutherland, is about Dennis the Menace and his dog Gnasher. It is a good example of a narrative work. It tells a story in a straightforward way, which also makes us laugh.

The story is told in a series of drawings, each contained in a box. The artist gives the feeling of movement by taking some of the action from one frame into the next. With their sense of motion, comics are like film and TV images.

The first frame has Dennis and Gnasher rushing towards us from an open door. Their feet and paws shoot out of the bottom of the picture, with clouds of dust streaming from their feet. The edge of the frame is a zig-zagging jagged line and the colours are very bright and strong. The whole picture has movement and energy, and this feeling continues throughout the rest of the story.

Comic books tell stories in a direct and visually exciting way, and it is this that makes them so popular.

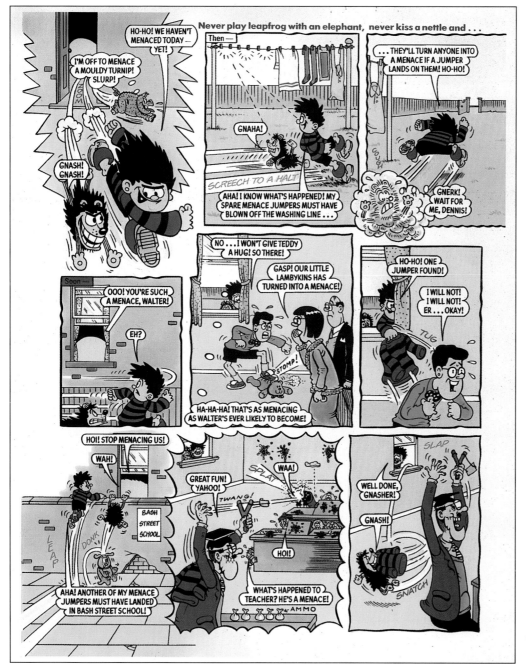

Dennis the Menace and Gnasher, 1995, by David Sutherland (born 1934), for *The Beano*. © D. C. Thomson & Co. Ltd.

Shona Kinloch was asked to make a fountain for the company that runs Scotland's nuclear power stations. Rather than tell a story about nuclear power using scientific images of atoms and machinery, she decided to be lighthearted and tell a joke about a very serious subject. She called the sculpture *Fission*, the name for a way of making nuclear power. The sculpture makes a joke on the name. She has used the fact that fission sounds like 'fish on' and has made a sculpture of three men with fish on their heads.

Producing the sculpture was a long process. First, the artist had to make a clay model of the sculpture. A mould was then made from this, and **molten bronze** was poured into the mould to make the finished piece. The forms Shona Kinloch uses in her work are usually soft and rounded, like the figures and fish shown here.

Shona Kinloch has used just one simple idea for her story, but it gives us a lot to think about: are we in favour of nuclear power; will it harm our environment; and even, will it kill fish?

Fission, 1993, by Shona Kinloch (born 1962), cast bronze, height 2m.
Collection: Scottish Nuclear PLC (the sculpture stands outside the headquarters in East Kilbride).

NICOLA ATKINSON-GRIFFITH

Captured, 1995, by Nicola Atkinson-Griffith (born 1962),
pencil on paper, metal. Collection: Art Machine 95.

Usually an artist tells only one story at a time.
In *Captured*, however, Nicola Atkinson-Griffith
has taken hundreds of stories, from people from
all over Scotland, and made them into one
enormous work. Each person's story is hand-
written by the artist and is made into a book.
The hundreds of books are then attached to the
walls of a room, filling it from floor to ceiling
so that we are completely surrounded by them.
The pages face outwards and, if we had time,
we could read every individual story. Suddenly,
as we stand looking, all the books begin to
move. The pages flap like butterflies' wings, the
writing becomes blurred and the sound of the
moving books fills the room. As this happens,
the hundreds of stories seem to merge in the
noise and movement.

The artist is not like a journalist, collecting
people's stories. Nor is she like a sculptor, who
uses shapes and forms. Rather, she is like a
poet, suggesting and hinting at the ideas she
wants to express.

In this **installation** the artist makes us think
about how people's personal stories become
part of the story of the whole community or
country they live in.

THOMAS FAED

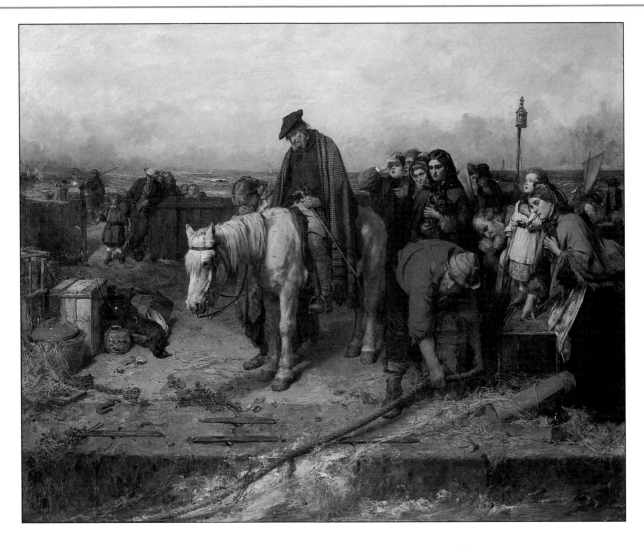

Last of the Clan, 1865, by Thomas Faed (1826–1900), oil on canvas, 145 x 183cm.
Collection: Glasgow Museums, Art Gallery and Museum, Kelvingrove.

In Victorian times, pictures that told stories were especially popular. People would visit art galleries in great numbers to see the latest painting, like Thomas Faed's *Last of the Clan*.

This story is about the Scots who were forced to leave their Highland villages and **emigrate** to America and Canada in the 1800s. This was known as the Highland Clearances. Faed was so interested in making sure that people understood what was happening in the picture that he placed these words beside it: 'When the steamer had slowly backed out, and John MacAlpine had thrown off the hawser [rope], we began to feel that our once powerful clan was now represented by a feeble old man and his daughter.'

Every detail has been carefully painted. Shiny pottery, scattered straw and rusty chains litter the quayside. The waves splash against the stone and the rope is pulled tight by the departing ship. The people's bowed heads and sad faces help to tell us about the hopelessness of those left behind. We cannot see the **emigrants** on the ship. The artist has left this part of the story to our imagination.

WILLIAM McTAGGART

The Highland Clearances are also the subject of this picture by William McTaggart. However, in *The Sailing of the Emigrant Ship*, the artist leaves almost everything to our imagination and seems to be more interested in showing us the fresh openness of a wind-blown **seascape**. McTaggart liked to paint out of doors, using actual places as subjects for his paintings. The whole picture has been made with strokes of paint placed quickly on to the canvas, giving us an **impression** of the scene rather than a detailed and realistic picture of what he saw.

The emigrant ship is sailing in a vast, endless sea under a huge sky filled with rolling clouds. There are people at the bottom of the picture who seem to be playing on the shore, but the artist has painted them as outlines, like ghosts or spirits left behind. The boat is just a distant speck on the **horizon**, but we can imagine the sadness of the people leaving their homeland. They are sailing into the unknown, leaving behind fond memories of happier times.

The Sailing of the Emigrant Ship, 1895, by William McTaggart (1835–1910), oil on canvas, 75 x 86cm. Collection: National Gallery of Scotland.

Dreams

As well as representing the real world, art can go beyond this and show us a world that is imagined. Some artists like to create strangely unreal images that make us question what we are looking at. Surrealist art often contains a weird mixture of subjects which do not appear to be connected with each other.

Symbolism uses real objects as symbols of ideas. In this type of art, people, places and things can look very realistic, but the artists may change the shapes and sizes, the colours or the light to make things seem odd and unusual. Even time and space can be mixed up. There are no limits to what is possible in our imagination.

CALUM COLVIN

Sacred Ibis, 1995, by Calum Colvin (born 1961), cibachrome photograph.
Collection: the artist.

Some artists enjoy playing tricks on our eyes and confusing our minds. In this picture, it is difficult to decide exactly what we are looking at. Is it a room full of furniture? Is it a big blue bird? Is it a sculpture or a painting? Calum Colvin mixes up flat shapes with three-dimensional forms, so that our idea of what is real and what is not becomes unclear.

In *Sacred Ibis*, our eyes follow the outline of a bird over a bed, across a guitar and through a teddy bear. Sometimes we see the bird; sometimes we see the objects in the room.

To produce such a complicated **illusion**, the artist painted over every surface in the room with strong, sometimes garish colours, carefully creating the shape of the bird. Finally, he took a photograph of the scene. This extraordinary vision of a huge bird with its curved beak and sharp talons filling a tiny, cluttered room leaves us unsure of what we are seeing.

ADRIAN WISZNIEWSKI

The whole process of making a work of art is difficult to explain but it always starts with the imagination. Thoughts and feelings flow through our minds until an idea begins to develop and becomes clearer. Artists enjoy playing with ideas, thinking about different combinations of images that might suit the picture they are working on.

In this **screenprint**, called *Po-et*, Adrian Wiszniewski shows us a person who is searching for inspiration. We see a poet with an open book in front of him. He is gazing dreamily into the distance, while above him float all the disconnected thoughts that are running through his mind. Mountains, a bridge and a strange, unravelling building are mixed up with trees, clouds and a log flying through the air. All of this is shown in bright primary colours against a dense, black background, as if the ideas are lighting up the darkness. The poet has created an imaginary landscape of thoughts drifting through space.

Po-et, 1986, by Adrian Wiszniewski (born 1958), screenprint, 139 x 106cm.
Collection: Adrian Wiszniewski and the Glasgow Print Studio.

35

BRIAN CONNOLLY

Modern technology has opened up many new ways of making visual art. Using video cameras and computers, artists can create images that we can be part of, as well as look at.

In *Ingress-Engress*, Brian Connolly and artists from Trongate Studios Glasgow use a large video screen to show a film of the room we are in. They create a fantasy world where strange images appear and disappear. The images are taken from eight TV monitors below the large screen, each showing someone's personal journey to a special place. On the screen we see ourselves moving around the room with other people, who come and go through closed doors. As we sit down, we sit inside another person's body. We stand up and we are under a giant waterfall. Cars and lorries drive through the room. One minute we are in a gym watching weight-lifters, the next on a beach with waves crashing on the shore around us. As these events unfold, we look around at the other people, and realize that there is no one else in the room. We are alone.

The artists are using technology to play with ideas of time and place. They create an illusion in which we have to question what is real or unreal. We can see ourselves in a dream-world, but are we part of it or are we still in a gallery?

Ingress-Engress, 1995, by Brian Connolly (born 1961) and artists from Trongate Studios Glasgow (A Project Ability Initiative), video. Collection: Art Machine 95.

JOHN MOONEY

Coming to a Head, 1989, by John Mooney (born 1948), watercolour, 58 x 80cm.
Collection: Edinburgh City Art Centre.

Using imagination can help us to create anything, and our dreams and fantasies can lead to some very surprising art. John Mooney's pictures are full of amusing ideas which are shown in perfect detail and painted with a great deal of patience and accuracy. The impossible images he invents appear to be solid and real, and yet they exist only in the artist's imagination.

In *Coming to a Head*, Mooney has taken a chimney, a cactus and a stone monument and combined them to make some peculiar-looking heads. Using all kinds of unexpected arrangements, he changes one object into another: the faces are made of plywood; a ball becomes an eye; the monument is a nose. Each structure is contained within a box and the whole composition is set out in a brightly-coloured grid, with each figure stranger than the last. The artist's visual tricks leave us to puzzle over what each new shape is, and to wonder what it all means!

MARGARET MACDONALD

Fairy tales, myths and legends have always been popular subjects with artists. In the days before television, films and videos, artists who made images of fantasy were very popular. At the beginning of the twentieth century, the city of Glasgow was famous in Europe for the art, design and architecture of people such as Charles Rennie Mackintosh and Margaret Macdonald. The way they worked was known as The Glasgow Style.

Margaret Macdonald was an artist with a rich and vivid imagination. As well as making drawings, paintings and embroideries, she produced designs in plaster and metal as decorations for furniture and houses. Her ghostly, dream-like figures of women, mermaids or

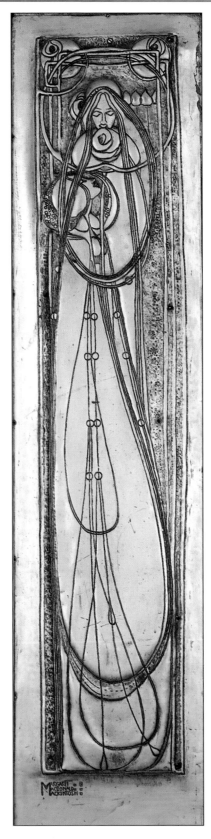

witches were often intertwined with flowers and leaves, long waving strands of hair, or flowing water in beautifully decorative designs.

Her metal panel, called *The Dew*, shows the figures of two sleeping women combined with the shapes of roses and teardrops, creating a strange, moonlit atmosphere of silent stillness. The picture suggests a magical fantasy in which people and nature merge and become one.

The Dew, 1901,
by Margaret Macdonald
(1864–1933), beaten silvered
lead, 122 x 30cm. Collection:
Glasgow Museums, Art Gallery
and Museum, Kelvingrove.

EDWARD BAIRD

Images have the power to create feelings and moods. A picture can give us a sense of warmth and happiness, or one of danger and unease. The title of the work, the way the scene is set and the artist's choice of colour can all affect our emotions.

Unidentified Aircraft by Edward Baird has an eerie feel. Painted during the Second World War, it shows a deserted, silent town beneath snow-covered hills. Three strangely similar faces look up to the sky from the bottom of the picture, and a hand is beginning to reach upwards. The people seem to be staring into the distance, searching for something unseen. There is no sign of an aircraft, only cotton-wool clouds in the dark blue sky.

The artist has created a strong atmosphere of uncertainty in his painting, which reflected people's fears of an enemy attack from the air during wartime.

Unidentified Aircraft, 1942, by Edward Baird (1904–49), oil on canvas, 71 x 91cm. Collection: Glasgow Museums, Art Gallery and Museum, Kelvingrove.

Glossary

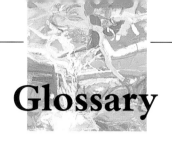

Abstract An image made of shapes, colours and textures, making no recognizable picture of the natural or physical world.

Atmosphere The general mood or feeling created in a work of art.

Balance When shapes, colours and forms are of equal importance throughout a work of art.

Bronze A metal mixture, or 'alloy', of tin and copper.

Brushstrokes Marks made with a paintbrush. These can be short, long, thick, thin, bold, delicate, fine, broad.

Canvas A strong cloth used as a base for oil paintings.

Cast To make something, like a sculpture, by shaping it in a mould.

Character The mixture of things that make up an individual, such as looks, moods and opinions.

Colour There are various ways of describing colour. These are some:

    primary – red, yellow and blue
    warm – such as red, pink, yellow, orange,
      brown
    cool – such as blue, green
    earthy – such as brown, yellow, ochre, grey
    descriptive words often used about colour
      – vivid, vibrant, bold, strong, bright,
      soft, pastel, pale, weak, light, flat

Compose To put together lines, shapes, forms and colours to make a work of art.

Composition The term used to describe the way all the shapes and forms in a work of art are put together.

Construction Usually a sculpture or something three-dimensional made up of several different parts.

Contrast The difference between two opposites, such as dark/light, rough/smooth or high/low.

Decorative Attracting attention by the use of extra shapes, patterns, colours.

Detail A small part of an artwork; or the smallest things that a work of art shows, like the lines of hair, the texture of cloth or the patterns on things.

Elegy A sad poem, usually to do with death.

Embroideries Images or patterns made by stitching thread into the surface of cloth.

Emigrant Someone who emigrates.

Emigrate To leave one's native country to live in another country.

Expressive A way of working in art that has to do with communicating feelings.

Form The roundness of something.

Graffiti Scribbled writing and slogans, usually done on walls.

Graphic Any kind of flat artwork, but usually refers to drawing.

Graphite A mineral, mined from the ground, which can be used for drawing. It is also used to make the 'lead' in pencils.

Harmony Where shapes or colours have a similar, usually pleasing, look about them.

Horizon The imaginary line in an image where the sky and the land or sea appear to meet.

Illusion Something that you think you can see, but is not there.

Image A picture or representation of something.

Impression An unclear image of something, usually produced very quickly and without much detail. This creates a feeling about the

subject rather than a realistic copy of it.
A group of French artists worked in this style in the late nineteenth century, and were called the Impressionists.

Inspiration Ideas and sources for works of art.

Installation One artwork that fills a whole room.

Landscape An outdoor scene.

Leviathan Something of great size.

Life-size The same size as in real life.

Likeness Looks like what it represents.
A portrait that is an accurate picture of what someone looks like is said to be a 'good likeness'.

Line The continuous mark made by a brush, pencil or stick.

Media The materials used by artists.

Molten The state of metal when it melts in the heat of a furnace.

Mood A general feeling created in a work of art.

Moulded Made into a shape by pressing or pouring material (metal, clay or wax) into another shape, or mould.

Narrative A work of art that tells a story.

Oil (paint) Powder paint mixed with linseed oil.

Pastel Crayons made from powdered colour and glue. They are dusty and soft to draw with.

Patron A person who buys work from an artist.

Pattern Produced by repeating the same shape, colour or line.

Portrait An image of a person.

Realistic Copying the appearance of something.

Relief A work of art made by taking material away from a flat surface or adding material to the surface.

Resin A plastic which, when liquid, can be cast in a mould. When it sets, it becomes very hard.

Sagas Ancient stories about the adventures of gods and heroes.

Scale The difference in size of one thing to another.

Screenprint A method of making many prints using a stencil stuck to a mesh or screen.

Sculpture A work of art in three dimensions, i.e., having height, width and depth.
A sculpture is usually worked from stone, clay, wood or moulded metal.

Seascape A picture of the sea.

Self-portrait An image of oneself.

Series A term used to describe a number of works on the same subject.

Shape The outline of an image.

Sketches Drawings, made quickly, often to record things the artist sees.

Snapshot A photograph, taken quickly.

Still life A work of art in which objects are used as the inspiration and subject.

Studies Detailed drawings made to help produce a finished artwork.

Style A particular way of working in art. Different artists can share the same style.

Subject The person, place, object and so on, that a work of art is about.

Textile A work of art made of cloth.

Texture The look or feel of a surface, i.e., rough, smooth, lumpy.

Three-dimensional Something with height, width and depth. Sculpture is three-dimensional.

Tone The level of light or dark.

Two-dimensional Something with height and width. Paintings and drawings are two-dimensional.

Watercolour (paint) Powder paint mixed with water.

Galleries and Museums to Visit

Aberdeen Art Gallery
Schoolhill
Aberdeen AB9 1FQ
Tel: 01224 646333

City Art Centre
2 Market Street
Edinburgh EH1 1DE
Tel: 0131 529 3993

The Dick Institute
Elmbank Avenue
Kilmarnock KA1 3BU
Tel: 01563 526401

Glasgow Museum and Art
Gallery
Kelvingrove
Glasgow G3 8AG
Tel: 0141 221 9600

The Glasgow Print Studio
22 King Street
Glasgow G1 5QP
Tel: 0141 552 0704

The Gracefield Studios
The Gracefield Arts Centre
28 Edinburgh Road
Dumfries DG1 1JQ
Tel: 01387 261234

The Hunterian Art Gallery
University of Glasgow
University Avenue
Glasgow G12 8QQ
Tel: 0141 339 8855

Inverness Museum and Art
Gallery
Castle Wynd
Inverness IV2 3ED
Tel: 01463 237114

Kirkcaldy Museum and Art
Gallery
War Memorial Gardens
Kirkcaldy, Fife KY1 1YG
Tel: 01592 260732

The Maclaurin Art Gallery
Rozelle Park,
Monument Road
Alloway,
Ayr KA7 4NQ
Tel: 01292 443708/445447

McLean Museum
15 Kelly Street
Greenock PA15 8JH
Tel: 01475 723741

McManus Gallery
Albert Square
Dundee DD1 1DA
Tel: 01382 432020

National Gallery of Scotland
The Mound
Edinburgh EH2 2EL
Tel: 0131 556 8921

Paisley Museum and Art
Gallery
High Street, Renfrewshire
Paisley PA1 2BA
Tel: 0141 889 3151

Perth Museum and Art
Gallery
78 George Street
Perth PH1 5LB
Tel: 01738 632488

The Pier Arts Centre
Victoria Street
Stromness
Orkney
Tel: 01856 850209

Scottish National Gallery of
Modern Art
75 Belford Road
Edinburgh EH4 3DR
Tel: 0131 556 8921

Scottish National Portrait
Gallery
1 Queen Street
Edinburgh EH2 1JD
Tel: 0131 556 8921

Smith Art Gallery and
Museum
Dumbarton Road
Stirling FK8 2RQ
Tel: 01786 471917

Summerlee Heritage Trust
West Canal Street
Coatbridge ML5 1QD
Tel: 01236 431261

Map of Scotland, including places listed
with galleries and museums to visit.

Key

Mountains

● Towns/cities

0   80km
0   50miles

SHETLAND

ORKNEY
Stromness ●

*NORTH
SEA*

LEWIS

NORTH UIST

BENBECULA

SOUTH UIST

RAASAY

SKYE

CANNA

BARRA

RUM

EIGG

COLL

TIREE

ULVA   MULL

*ATLANTIC
OCEAN*

JURA

ISLAY

ARRAN

● Inverness

● Aberdeen

S C O T L A N D

Dundee ●

Perth ●

Stirling ●   Kirkcaldy ●

Greenock ● Glasgow ●
                              Edinburgh ●
Paisley ● Coatbridge ●

● Kilmarnock

Ayr ●

Dumfries ●

E N G L A N D

I R E L A N D

Further Information

Books to read

The Bigger Picture by Andrew Gibbon Williams and Andrew Brown (BBC Books, 1993)

Contemporary Painting in Scotland by Bill Hare (Craftsman House, 1993)

Faces by Christopher McHugh (Wayland, 1992)

The History of Western Painting by Juliet Heslewood (Belitha Press, 1993)

I Like Painting by Melanie and Chris Rice (Kingfisher Books, 1989)

People at Work by Christopher McHugh (Wayland, 1993)

Scottish Art, 1460-1990 by Duncan Macmillan (Mainstream Publishing, 1995)

Scottish Art Since 1900 edited by Keith Hartly (National Galleries of Scotland, 1989)

Stories in Art by Clare Gogerty (Cherry Tree Books, 1994)

Town and Country by Christopher McHugh (Wayland, 1993)

BBC Education Scotland has produced the unit of programmes, *Looking at Scottish Art*, in the television series *Around Scotland* (transmission: Autumn 1995).

Information on ordering print support material is available from:

BBC Education Scotland, Room 305, 5 Queen Street, Edinburgh EH2 1JF.

Telephone: 0131 469 4262.

Index